Can I Eat That?

For my sons, Auggie Behr and Achilles Bug
JDS

For Clydey-cakes, Love, Tati
JR

Phaidon Press Limited
Regent's Wharf
All Saints Street
London N1 9PA

phaidon.com

First published 2016
© 2016 Phaidon Press Limited
Text copyright © Joshua David Stein
Illustrations copyright © Julia Rothman

Artwork illustrated using ink and gouache.

ISBN 978 0 7148 7110 3 (UK edition)
008-1215

A CIP catalogue record for this book is available from the British Library. All rights reserved. No part of this publication may be reproduced, stored in a retrieval system or transmitted, in any form or by any means, electronic, mechanical, photocopying, recording or otherwise, without the written permission of Phaidon Press Limited.

Designed by Meagan Bennett

Printed in China

> A portion of the proceeds of this book will be donated to Action Against Hunger, a global humanitarian organization committed to ending world hunger.

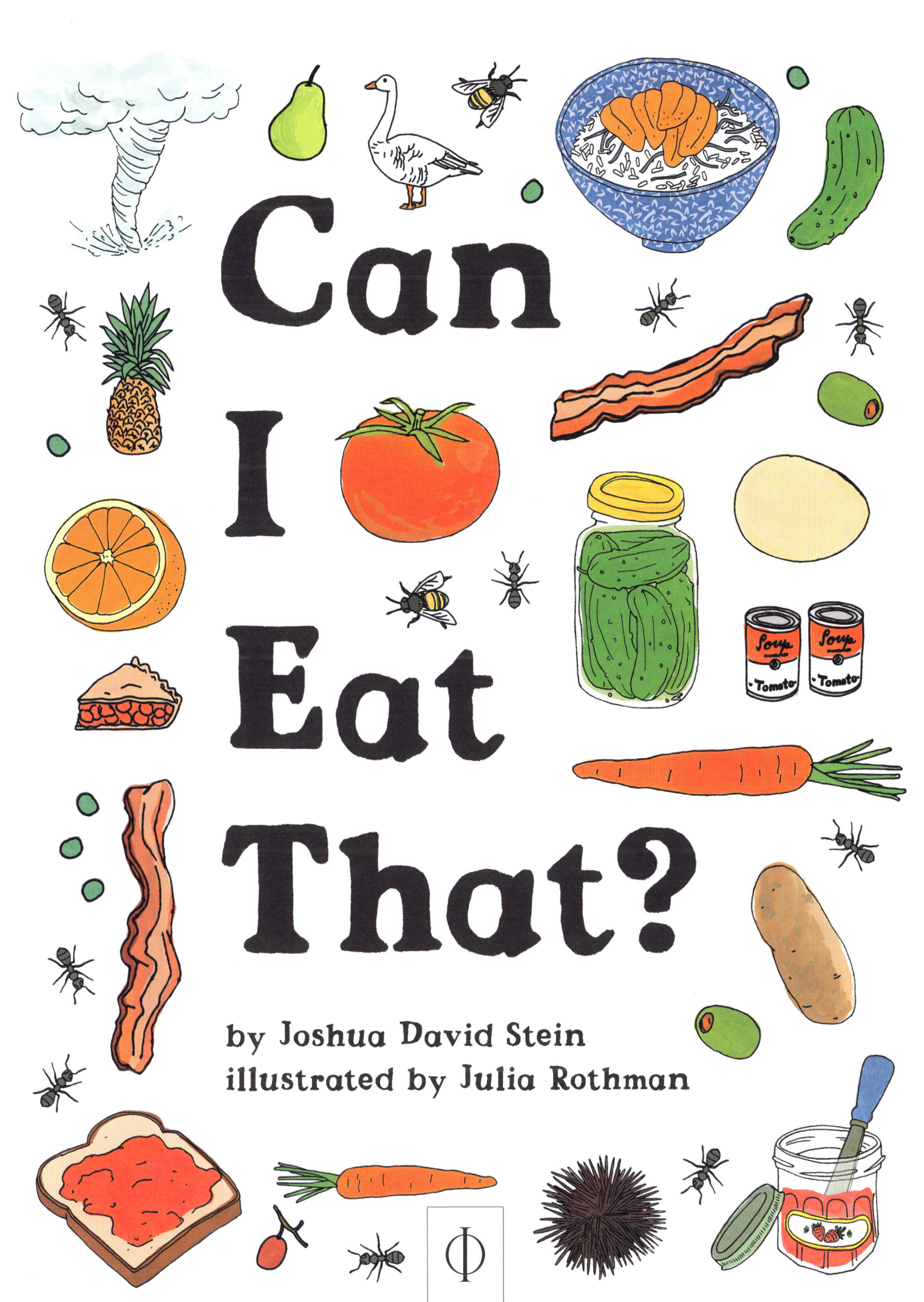

an orange?

an olive?

a sea urchin?!

Yes! You can eat all three!

A sea urchin is called *uni* in Japanese.

Inside the *uni* are bright orange strips of meat called coral. You can serve the coral on rice. *Uni donburi!*

a potato?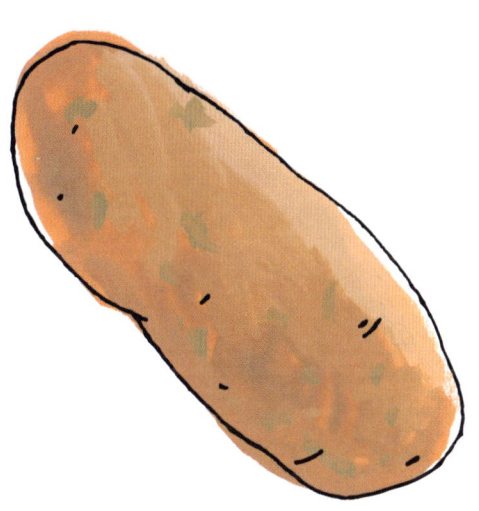

 a tomato?

a tornado?!

No, you can't eat a tornado!
It's made out of wind.

But you *can* eat . . .

tonnato, a sauce
from Italy made
with tuna . . .

Can we go pickle picking some time?

Not exactly.

Pickles are really vegetables that have been soaked in vinegar or in a salty water called brine. Pickled cucumbers, or gherkins, are a popular kind of pickle. There are many flavours to choose from!

I eat jelly...

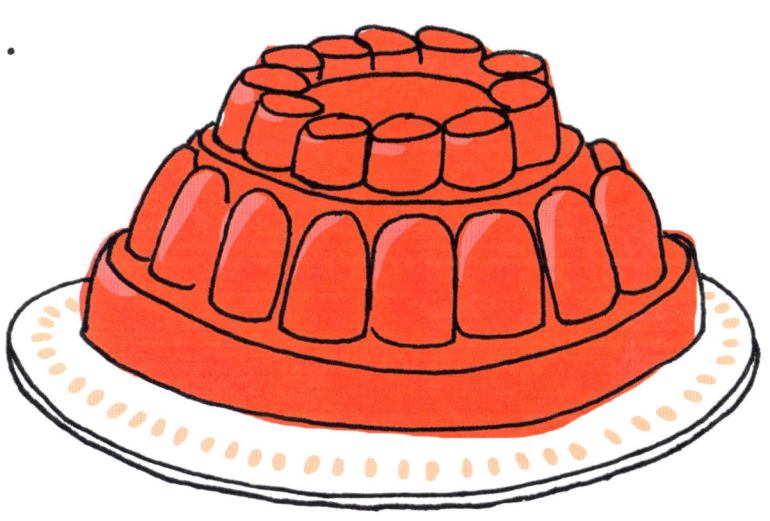

and I eat fish...

can I eat jellyfish?!

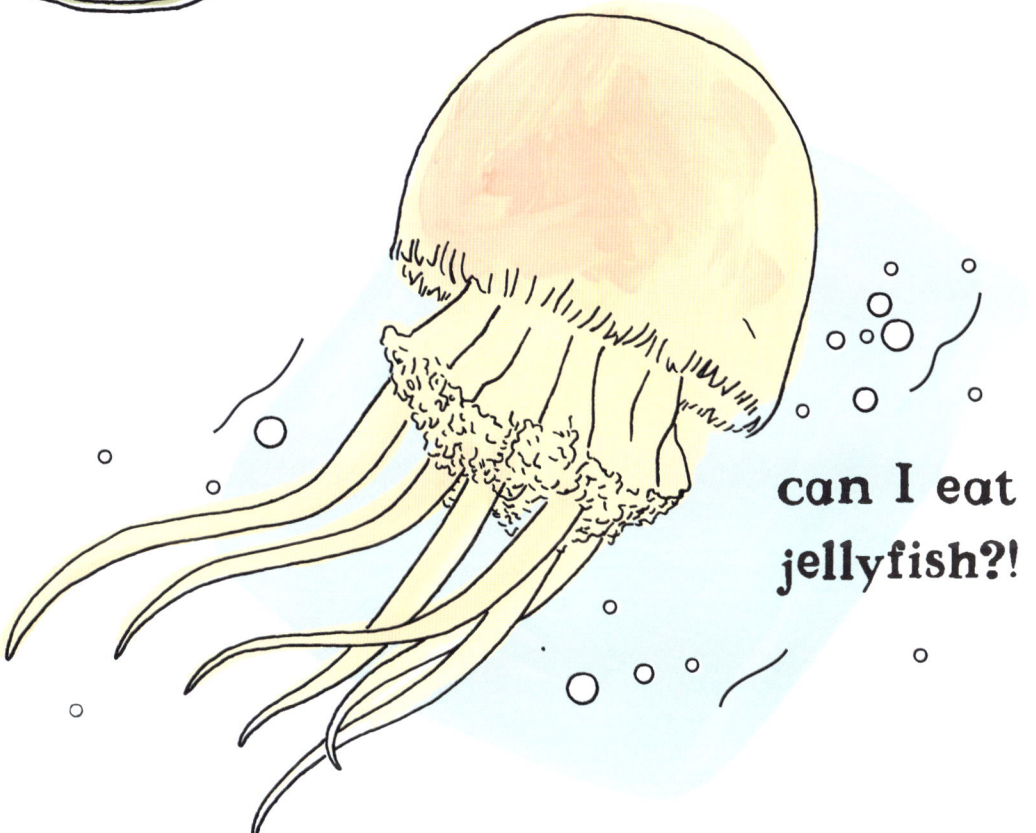

Actually, you can!

In China, jellyfish is thinly sliced and served cold with shredded vegetables.

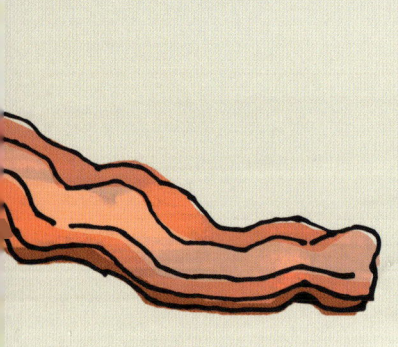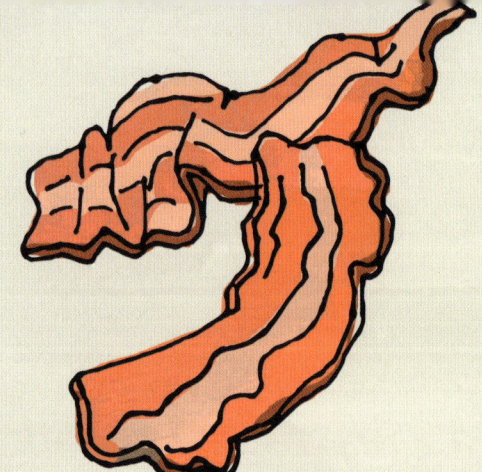

If there is...
BACON
is there...
BACOFF?

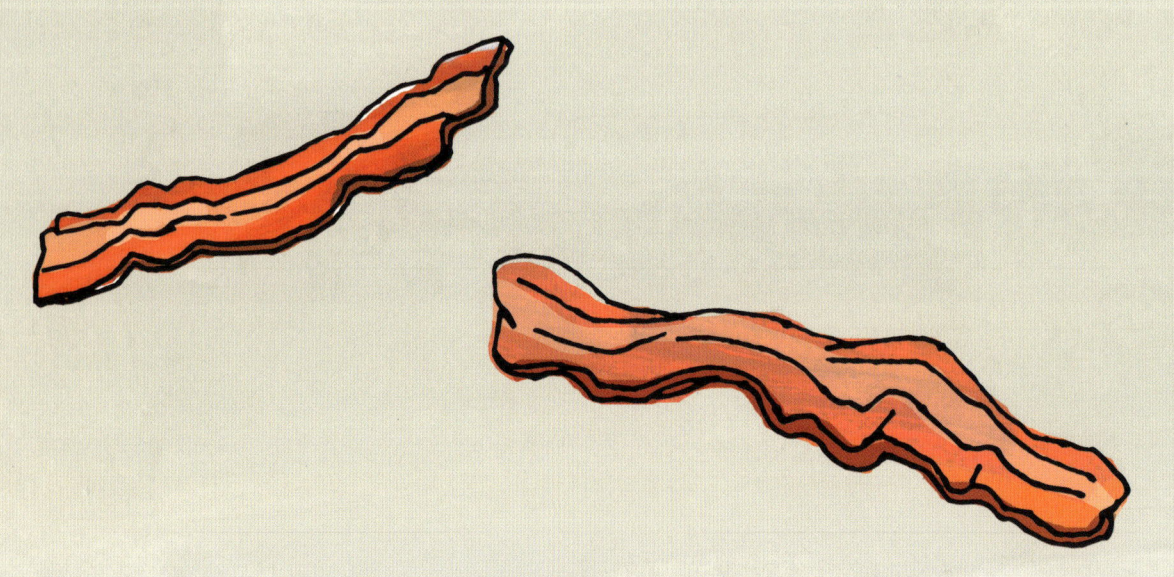

If there is...
KETCHUP
is there...
KETCHDOWN?

If there is a...
RAISIN
is there a...
RAISOUT?

Is this a
faraway lime
or a
life-sized pea?

Is this a
distant doughnut
or a
close-up Cheerio?

Do fish have fingers?

No. Fish have fins, but they don't have fingers.

What we call fish fingers are actually fried bits of fish. But they are called fingers because they look like our fingers. Kind of.

Do eggs grow on eggplants?

No! Eggplant is another name for aubergine.

Oh. Where do eggs come from then?

Chickens.

OK, and where do chickens come from?

All chickens come from eggs, but not all eggs become chickens.

Some eggs become breakfast.

Can I Eat?